shadows cast

sm heal

BookLeaf Publishing

India | USA | UK

Presentation by *BookLeaf Publishing*

Web: www.bookleafpub.com

E-mail: info@bookleafpub.com

ISBN: 9789358316933

First edition 2023

my light, my life, my love

ACKNOWLEDGEMENT

all of the women in my life who fight for me and hear me, even when I can't fight for myself or see into my true self, I honor you. ali- thank you for reminding me that things that scare us can also rebuild us and for your honest feedback- don't start with a positive haha. my mom and my sister who are there always. my dad who helped me understand that poetry can just be.

enough resilience

angry echoes of where I should

    have been

who I, with enough resilience, could

    have been

mirrored in age, reflecting time

of what I never

    have been

resurgent justice

resurgence of your growling temper
suffer restless nights
reveling- rousing and rustling
of our gruff encounters

grounded, solely
by the Justice
of your words

fucking go away

i miss that taste
the flicker-
flight which hovers-

ensure- ensnare
you envelop it
know that it can never-
fucking go away

now, try reading that back up

closure

the final swipe of cement
      covering yesteryear's transgressions
      running forward
         without waiting for
            that paint to dry

   denying ourselves
      the nesting purgatory
         of transition

vyings

5

wanderlust overwhelms the serenity of secure
ideals, challenging identity with savory outcome
of Hedonistic self-indulgence, unrest from
the leaf rustlings within… charge forth defying
acceptance and heroic vyings force
what only the idealistic youthful flock
will render of a global entity denying
Zealous Pride

the flow

the flow
     the gliding of gargantuan dreams
  as they slither, entwining around
     my ankles, like the ocean's salty
embrace

waiting, yearning to ease me out
  farther, away from the solid
    into, the upheaval

wickery hallways

wickery hallways
filled with juxtaposition
       and argumentative
       semantics
leave lingering embraces
       of flirtation mingling
with tantric conversation
       of notwithstanding
         youthful zest
       equate princely ideals
       with 'Trumpian realism'
         to find that the only

True knowledge is that
 simply
  quietly
   lustfully
    of one's own self

endless moment

angry postulations
of Aphrodite lusts
hindered by hopelessness
enduring
towards the inevitable end
   of lackadaisical days

this hopeless yearns
for the spiciness of
a life still to be lived
in the wantonness of
nothing to come…

because the hopefulness
that just maybe
for this singular
spirit of time, you,
and those enigmatic
eyes, and your softly perfect lips
could- with hope-
be just mine
for that singular, endless
   moment

future generations

malfeasance wrought by the
    effervescent allure of pretension

guides future generations toward
    a life, not of their
  choosing, but of the chains
brought by expectation

tipping point

t

 i

  pp

   ing

       poi

        nt

         of a soul's light

dimming others as we are dimmed

          the shadows cast on our

light

          not knowing where ours

          begins and anothers ends
          until the darkness is full

kettle shrills

11

I am not the pot calling the kettle black

                        I am too aware of my
own transgressions

the whistle of my kettle shrills

          sometimes

               scalding me with its truths

A stranger's held gaze

A glimmer
  that shimmer down my
    left side
 A lil flit-flut
   tug at my right
    side memory
A curl's cast dawning on my lips

  remembrance's warmth
  awakening
And all it took was
  a stranger's held gaze
  across a room

tiptoe around

that Puck's twitch flickers
upon those supple lips
smirking
tiptoe
around
all that is unsaid

rolling gales brew within
in anticipation of what
your next move will be

defeat is at hand

ancient track

its wetness slides so easily
        like it's got this memory of
    this ancient track
        unused for sometime, but
        well trodden

its origins the same- this
    hopeless abyss
    its destination spread
        among the unending agony

timber

there's a certain timber

       to

          the

    shriek

       of

      first contact

with snow melt water

its

  echo

      chills

        the bystander

even as they double over in laughter

  of the other's pain

promise

even embers sparkle
    the whispering promise
of something more, something
    actually worth shit

  that mercurial promise
drowned by whiskey's
    evensong

drowned by a mental
      numbness of technological overload

drowned by whispers of

yesterday's promise

cardinal

no matter which direction
  sadness seeps in
the indelible southern yearning
  for that deep syncopation
the western sparkle in my heart
  that spreads through
  my chest & into my stomach
the north void- the knowing void
  of how that feeling can
  feel
and without it, the darkness is
  deeper- lonelier- emptier

How can you feel emptier than empty?

syncopation

delicate butterfly wings

flapping

hello to me

in the soft breeze

then the wind picks up,

it stays with me,

but its wings

shift &

shutter-

move in syncopation

the still calms return

and I can't tell if it is

soothed by the missing wind-
or disappointed

closure

closure

the final swipe of cement
        covering yesteryear's transgressions
        running forward
                without waiting for
                        that paint to dry

    denying ourselves
        the nesting purgatory
            of transition